ASCEND OUT OF NIGHT

NEW AND SELECTED POEMS

by

Lucius DuBose

Swan Creek Books
2017

Swan Creek books is the publishing arm of DuBose Graphics, an independent printmaking studio established in 1977 for the creation and distribution of Lucius DuBose's hand printed and hand colored original etchings. "Swan Creek" refers to the stream by that name that flows through Lewis County, Tennessee, described on pages 63 - 64 of Re-imagining God, A Spiritual Journey, *by Lucius DuBose.*

Published by Swan Creek Books, Nashville, Tennessee.

Printed in the United States of America

ISBN: 978-0-692-83753-5

To Printha McCallum, my beloved step-daughter,
without whom none of this would have reached
the printed page . . . .

PREFACE

What better preface to this collection of verse than this quote from a great American poet and teacher of the art, the late, John Hall Wheelock:

> "A poem does not originate out of an impulse to communicate. A poem is what happens when a poet rediscovers for himself, the reality we have lost sight of because, to use Shelley's metaphor, it has been overlaid by the veil of familiarity. The process, however, is not one of rediscovery and subsequent transmittal in a poem. The poem itself is part of the discovery. In making it, the poet learns what it is that he has rediscovered. Thus, a child, when it begins to speak, learns what it is that it knows. And a child will talk to itself, with no one around to hear, so in the poem the poet, it might be said, is talking to himself. He has established communication with his own being, and therefore potentially with others."

What is Poetry?, John Hall Wheelock.
Charles Scribner and Sons. New York. 1963. page 27.

CONTENTS

ASCEND OUT OF NIGHT

Descend out of light to the lapping edge,
to the ridge of the wintered sand,
a flexed forearm veined by parried waves.
Go down to the man dark,
sky light-works, where Sirius
brightly bays the hunter lost
in star forests of the night,
and Betelgeuse lays down the sea
a red light carpet to the water steps.

Ascend, ascend out of night
as dark concedes the east.
At sun's break in the last wet desert
will appear in last earth print,
for those who wait, a butterfly
half buried in the sand.

LOOKING BACK

. . . he had set his course, a life
that he would patent for himself,
a world of . . .
penetrable boundaries,
a lifetime of . . .
ever moveable
horizons.

SYNESTHESIA

What was it then that so disturbed
the natural consequence of time,
the way a breeze cut through the screen
and grazed bare feet on a bedspread pushed back?
(what was I thinking just before that wind?)
an odor typical of a time of year
that mingled with the dry-mouth
dread of narrowing tomorrows?
What combination of sensations unexpected
triggered this random coalescence
of reconstructed sixty year old myths?
What takes me back, an unwanted
instant transmigration?

It is another room, some other house
than this today, and long ago;
another time, a visit. Whose place is this:
two stories, nineteen-twenties stucco style?
I can't recall a smell.
(or could I if it came? Was it that, unrecognized,
that brought these pictures back?)
There was a rug upstairs
where my father had a room,
(What was he doing there?
Fathers are supposed to have
whole houses of their own,
not single rooms in strangers'),
a woolen runner in the hall,
until it jogged down steep turned stairs.

And on threadbare parade
a wooden soldier tried to march,
his tunic worn to grain by
someone else's hand, someone not there.
Whose was that rigid little man?
He would not march for me;
we weren't in tune.

That's all I can remember, save
the lawn not played on, and
the curving street (was there
a sidewalk? Yes, I think . . .).

There must have been there, too,
this certain quality of wind
to tickle a child's bare foot,
and the smoky taste of unspelt fears,
in a place cut loose from yesterday.
Is this the place? Are we going to stay?
And can there be tomorrow in a land
of someone else's things,
never in your own backyard?
There are no beds that stay and smell like you.
Lady can't have her litters here;
She won't know where to go.
This is no place, a temporary set;
this neighborhood's made no pledge to me
to stay the same.

And then the breeze, a soft spring wind
from home, blown all the way
to reassure connections - some things hold -
a token, touchstone for an alien child.

This afternoon it serves connections, too;
this certain touch, smell, temperature
of breath that strikes me in a certain pose,
at a moment of peculiar dread, wipes out all time.
The alien child and I are one,
still looking for a place;
but in my father's rented rooms
the wooden soldier will not march for me.

<u>THOCK!</u>
(OR, WHY I NEVER MADE THE PGA)

I was about nine; it was
one of those southern summer days
when the sun conspires with kids
to stay up late . . . light enough to
"play out after supper".

I was in the neighborhood park
to give the slide another go,
making it fast with waxed paper
from a loaf of *Merita Bread*,

when this other kid showed up
with a golf ball and a club
(a five iron, I think it was).
I didn't know him;
he was younger than me.

He started knocking the ball
around, or trying to.
"Can I try it?" I asked,
thinking to show him how.
It was the first time I had ever
held a real golf club.

I put the ball down, and
took my stance to knock
that thing across the park.
I drew back, and that was when
I heard the *Thock!*

and a cry of pain.

The club head caught him
on the brow, just above his eye
Thock! that's precisely the sound
a five iron makes in contact
with a kid's hard head;
Thock! that sound is engraved
upon my memory of that day.

Turning around, I saw red . . .
Blood. Lots of it, pouring into
his eye and down his face.
"Oh, Darn! I hit you in the eye".
I don't know why I said that.
He thought I had knocked
his eye out and made him blind.

He ran off , screaming, home.
I didn't know what to do.
But it was getting dark,
so I went home, too,
scared to death that I was
in real trouble. I wasn't.

No one blamed me;
It was an accident.
Once he was cleaned up
and the bleeding stopped,
a couple of stitches fixed his brow,
no permanent damage done.

Years later I took up golf
as a recreational sport.
I bought clubs. I learned the
proper stance and grips and
how to keep my eye on the ball.

I played for six or seven years with
little or no success. I never could
control my drives, or make the ball
go where I aimed. I think now
my backstroke was my nemesis.

Somehow, whenever I took
my club back for a swing
some part of me was tensing up,
Just waiting for the
Thock!

BIBLIOPHILE

A bibliophile born
in a bookless home,
of pageless parents,
book shelves bare cupboards.

Childhood diet of *Mother Goose*,
illustrated *Bible Story Book*,
Walt Disney Comics, *Big Little Books*,
tastes of the printed story.

A ripening hunger for pages,
paragraphs, chapters,
in third grade, school library
my brave new world.

Then weekly allowances,
saving nickels to buy my own,
measuring my wealth by the volume.

As I still do;
The house where I live a cave
walled with books.

I am exceedingly rich.

A SCRAPBOOK

A scrapbook,
cheap, dime-store bought,
with cardboard covers,
construction paper pages.

Belonging to my brother,
a junior high school project,
tossed aside, forgotten,
once it passed the grade.

I found it one day
in the room we shared,
curious to know what
he had been collecting.

Nothing much, it seemed;
just a scrapbook full
of colored pictures cut
from old *Life* magazines.

But all pictures of art
I'd never seen the likes of,
paintings by artists whose
names I'd never heard.

I was Art ignorant, save
for Bible story pictures,
Mother Goose, comics,
traditional portraits and the like.

Here were paintings by
Grant Wood, Reginald Marsh,
Thomas Hart Benton, Edward
Hopper, Charles Sheeler,

Paul Cadmus, John Steuart
Curry, each inviting me
to see the world through
his peculiar eyes.

Just a cheap scrapbook . . . ?
A revelation . . . a dawning . . .
a new specie of perception . . .
a passport to a new country . . .
to a personal future . . . .

INDEPENDENCE DAY

A month in a new place,
new city, new state,
neighborhood, new house -
no, not a house, an apartment -
not yet a home.

The novelty losing its edge,
strange rooms slow to earn
familiarity to a ten year old,
feeling caged, grieving for
what was left behind:

the dog, the ducks, a backyard
as big as a child's imagination,
the tree house, dirt to dig in,
his own attempt at growing things,
now never to be harvested.

So? the war years, lots of relocations
to alien towns, unfamiliar places . . .
just takes a little getting used to . . . .
But no, to this child, a sentence -
for the duration - to a life indoors.

That red brick and concrete H
(Hanover Court, apartment 2C
second floor back) offered no out-of-doors
outside his door, that he could claim,
where he might rehearse his childhood dreams.

But in the building's basement -
neglected since the movers put it there -
the instrument of his salvation:
a hand-me-down, red and white, 1940s,
single speed, balloon-tired, Schwinn Deluxe, Bicycle.

The day he pumped the tires up,
to put it to the test on city streets,
was the day he became the owner
of his where. . . the prince of speed
in getting to . . . wherever.

No longer ruled by circumstance,
he took possession of his freedom,
assumed command of his deciding,
cracked open his world, and
sent confining horizons reeling.

Highland Avenue, out front, became
his take-off runway to adventure;
he had set his course: a life
that he would patent for himself,
a world of
penetrable boundaries,
a lifetime of
ever moveable
horizons.

A VERY TOLERANT DOG

Like the furnace, like
the single car garage, and
like the oak trees in the yard,
she just came with the house.
A mix of whippet and terrier
(she was one fast pup),
her name was *Smudge*.

She wasn't our dog; she
did not belong to us. We
belonged to her, the third
family who agreed to pay -
dogfood, warm bed and playtime -
for the privilege of living
in her house.

The first of her families took her
away when they moved out, but,
like *Lassie*, she came home,
walking ten to fifteen miles
across the city, over Red Mountain,
her inner compass showing the way.

She had made herself at home
with our predecessors, and
now she made herself at
home with us. All in all,
a very tolerant dog, she
took no exceptions to our
residing in her house.

She grew old with us,
and when she died,
we buried her - with her
permission, of course -
in her own
backyard.

A LOT OF SINGING

For Christmas? What do I want?
Here's what I'd really like:
to be invited to sing the bass solo
in a Handel's *Messiah* sing-along.
That'll never happen, I know,
but it would be a thrill, because,
well, I just love to sing,
almost anything.

I was introduced to singing early on.
My mother played the ukelele,
and sang us lots of silly songs.
And I grew up in the Thirties
and Forties, when popular music
was singable, not like today
(my brother wanted so badly
to be the next Bing, or Perry,
or Frank; he took voice lessons,
and he tended to his hair a lot).

And, of course, we sang a lot in church;
The Old First Church in Birmingham.
I joined the adult choir
when I was just sixteen. I was
a bass, and hardly five feet tall.
Our director was a Swede named
Mr. Skoog. We had a paid quartet
to do the solo work and keep us
amateurs on key. We sang some
very good music, and we sang it . . .

well . . . pretty well.

About that time three other
guys and I formed a quartet
we called *The Fishmarket Four.*
You know, First Tuna, Second Tuna,
Barracuda, and Bass. I was
the Barracuda. We made one record
for some girls in Selma,
and one public appearance at
a Future Farmers convention in
Tuscaloosa. We were awful
but we had a lot of fun.

There were memorable songs
back then, with memorable lyrics.
Remember, *I'll Be Seeing You . . .*
and *We'll Meet Again . . .*
sad songs of the war years.
Then came the romantic ballads
of Nat King Cole, Sinatra,
The Four Freshmen, Doris Day,
Jo Stafford . . . . In the Sixties
We sang along with Joan Baez,
The Kingston Trio, Peter, Paul and Mary,
Bob Dylan, who warned us that
the times they were a'changing.

And they did. But the old songs
still sound good, and they're
still fun to sing (and if you've
forgotten the words, you can
look them up on line).
When my beloved Lenda was
dying, I sat one afternoon by
her bed in the Hospice room,

held her hand, and sang for her
all the old love songs I could
remember. I got one last smile
as a reward.

I still sing a lot out loud to
myself, probably more now
that I live alone, with no one
else to bother. It's good therapy.
And, you know, I think my old
singing voice might be coming back.

So, if you're looking for
a bass (or a barracuda)
for a sing-along,
give me a call.

RITUALS

In grade school the thing was
to kick the same rock
the whole way in the morning,
and all the way back in the afternoon.
If you could do that, then
the day was pretty much complete,
and what might happen in between:
grammar, long division, the uneven games
at recess, weren't so bad.

At fifteen you needed to *stamp*
every '47 Studebaker you saw
(to *stamp* you lick your thumb,
and touch your palm,
and smack it with your fist;
a boy's way of counting,
not bothering with the sum).
It seemed reassuring, you're not sure why;
having to do with control, you suppose,
like being in charge of keeping up
with all the newest cars.

And why should things change at this late date?
So, when you take your morning walk
you never change the route;
down the same streets, around the same blocks,
making sure to touch with both your feet
every single cement sidewalk square,

‘cause, if you’re true, and do not veer,
maybe they won’t have to go back in
and open up your heart again.

MILITARY ASPIRATIONS

An old snapshot from a box of recollections,
taken by some unremembered friend . . . of me,
in the Christmas parade in my college town,
marching at the head of Company D
of the college's R.O.T.C.,
Holding a Cadet Captain's rank.

I wore the Army's dress uniform of the time:
billed hat, olive drab *blouse* (the word
in military nomenclature for a short dress coat),
with brass buttons, over a khaki shirt
and tie, pants a special gray that
gave them the popular name of *pinks*.

My white gloves fairly glowing, and
across my chest a polished leather
Sam Brown Belt, from which hung
the scabbard of the ceremonial saber that was
upright against my shoulder at the *carry*
position in the saber manual-of-arms.

Returning to that placid post-war time, seeing
the uniform again, feeling the drum-beat's
quick-step cadence, the pride in a Company
well-drilled . . . recalling where it all had started:
age sixteen, high school R.O.T.C., when my M-1
rifle was almost as tall as I was . . .

I now knew that it was on that snapshot's day
that I had actually fulfilled my military dream.

My soldier's aspirations added up to that:
a handsome uniform, commanding a well trained
Company that marched in perfectly aligned
formation, if only as a vanguard for Santa's sleigh,

my only desired weapon a ceremonial saber,
too dull to inflict any sort of damage
on any non-existent foe.

AN UNNAMED CHILD

Imagine being told at thirty-six years old
that the name you've always gone by
wasn't yours - at least as far as bureaucratic
records were concerned.

My request for a copy of the record of my birth
had elicited a document - all vital stats correct -
my parents' names, the date, the place. But,
on the bottom line: *an un-named child.*

Un-named? Unreal. By state decree I wasn't me,
or, by omission, who I thought I was. I had
been *no one* all along. So, where did that leave
this nameless being who occupied my skin?

I didn't feel like someone else, and mirrors
saw no change; so, perhaps what seemed a pall upon
my whole biography was really a peculiar gift,
the chance to be whomever I now chose to be.

Ten dollars, a filled out form (no blanks, please)
and a Notary Public's imprint, and I could be
a whole new me. I would never have to answer again
to my Grand Dad's funny sounding name.

I could be Tom, or Bob, or Bill, have a middle
name, or not . . . take a President's name . . . maybe Harry?

Or my favorite Artist's . . . how does John James
Rembrandt sound? The possibilities were endless.

And there was the problem, too many choices.
That's probably why society lets the parents decide
(I only wish that mine had filled in all the blanks).
Well, in the end I took the simplest path.

I mailed my dollars and my duly notarized
official form to the South Carolina Bureau of
Vital Statistics, and I became whom I had
always been: Lucius Beddinger DuBose . . .
no longer an un-named child.

CONVERSATION

I got those yesterday, he said,
they hurt.

Those scratches?, I asked,
How?

On a wall, he said.

What were you doing?, I asked.

Climbing it, he said.

Of course, I said,
what else can you do with a wall?

You could tear it down, he said.

You're right, I said,
you could tear it down.

THE TRIUMPH OF THE CHILD

When I was a child,
I spoke like a child,
I thought like a child,
I saw like a child.
Then I became a man,
and I gave up childish ways.

But not so fast.
That child I put away
to his banishment never did accede,
nor freely choose to abdicate his throne.
An exiled king the lad remained,
a waiting prince on an off-shore isle,
for the reigning season's sure return.
From afar he kept his counsel close,
though now and again a childish chirp
to let me know he was still around.
Mostly he's waited and certainly smiled
at the parade of pretenders who postured up
to try and take his place.

Before the man the adolescent showed,
uniformed in the standard dress
of youthful freedom's rebellious demands,
an ungainly prince proudly preening
his unruly self-esteem, and pouring out
a grand cascade of premature beliefs
to fill the hole of absent certainties.

And all the while the child looked on
from afar, bemused, and said,
Oh, my, he sounds a lot like me.

But soon the grown-up took control;
That's me, I said, *I'm in the driver's seat!*
I've earned my place, the rest is up to me.
I'll go it on my own from here.

So, how did it go?
Well, not as self-determined
as the man had thought. You see . . .
I am - it's clear at this ripe age -
as once I was when I was newly here.

I did as I was taught to do back then,
or else what I was driven to;
I loved as I was loved, or not;
I chanced to fall in love with the love
I needed from the start;
I fathered as I had been fathered,
or to make up for what I'd missed;
and as for work, at last I settled down
to what this boy had always loved to make.

And now that the exit sign's in view,
my usher is still that same bright boy
who's always been my guide.
I've really come to like that kid.
So, I'll trust my hand in his to show the way,
as I did once to the school house door.

In the evening of a long, long day
the child comes home
to claim his fatherhood.

INIQUITIES REVISITED

Forgiveness does not seek excuses.
Forgiveness happens, sometimes
when the truth is so awful
that there simply is
nothing else that
one can do.

INIQUITIES REVISITED

. . . for I the Lord your God am a jealous God,
visiting the iniquity of the fathers upon the
children to the third and fourth generations . . . .
Exodus 20: 5 (RSV)

You will do, or not,
what I tell you to,
or not to do.

Those were the terms
of the contract my father
endeavored to force on me.
For his part, he would
work hard - he did -
to provide me the basics:
food, clothing, shelter.
The frills - defined as such by him -
were bargaining chips
for purchasing my behavior.
I would do as *he* thought best,
what *he* believed I ought to do,
or pay the price.

The price, early on,
a reminder with
the bite of a leather belt
on skinny little legs . . .

as well as other more subtle threats:
You *will* take part in the church's
Christmas play . . . (my stage fright
at age seven seemed not to count)
if you want to see that red truck
under the tree.

I learned the rules quite well,
that love was a commodity one must buy,
and deceit, thereby, a useful tool.
A mere imitation of goodness would
do quite well to keep him off my back.

It was a deal with the devil
that I worked out with my dad
(unknown to him, of course).
For me it was survival.
I would keep my real self hidden;
he would see a *charade* of
innocent behavior. It was
a trade-off in which the main
victim was the truth. But it
seemed to suit his brand
of love O. K. It became the
pattern of our life.

Before I left his house for good
one last transaction sealed
our epitaph: home from college
with cigarettes. I was ordered
to give them up, or else
give up my education.

If I did not obey, he would withhold
my tuition. He meant it, and,
having no choice, I promised . . . ,
knowing full well that on
the train back to school
I could purchase
a full fresh pack
of Lucky Strikes.

Poor man, he never knew
that he had lost the game
before it had begun, or that I
was playing by a different set of rules.
The self I kept to myself,
protected against invasion -
his mostly - he never would know.
He would not have been interested
anyway. To him I was just

a complicated problem, a rebel;
not a beloved son in whose
successes he took any joy.
He was dead to my liveliness.
The only voice he seemed to hear
was his own. And he had not
much to say, at least
not much to me.

I am left to wonder
what his father did to him . . .
whose father
was not there for him . . .

whose father
could not . . .
whose father . . .
et cetera . . .
et cetera . . .
et cetera . . .
to the third
and fourth
generations . . . .

SO SAD A STORY

I was just out of the car, when,
like a wounded bull he charged,
hemorrhaging hatred with an angry intensity
that promised to drag us both into
a black hole from which
no recollected love,
no filial memories
could ever
save us.

He was my father;
I was his second son.
I had made life changing decisions
he did not approve.
I bore him no
ill will.

I had come to explain,
to solicit his celebration,
but not his approval.
To that
he had no
right.

It is an amazing thing
to be told by your own father that (his words)
he hates everything you.
represent.

How could I get my mind around
the declaration that I was no longer
wanted in his
home?

How could I swallow the bitter pill,
that I would never be accepted (his words)
as one deserving of
my heritage?

How could I watch unscathed
as he hacked away with
unsheathed contempt
at all the ties that
bound?

How could my heart stay whole,
unbroken by
my father's
curse?

He did not speak to me
for the next six years, and
when we spoke at last - even
in the same room - it was
from miles apart.
We never
really met
again.

He died alone . . .
from me. He had
murdered our love, and
in so doing
cut himself off . . .
forever
from his
own
son.

HAVE YOU LOST YOUR FAITH?

"Have you lost your faith?"

I had no answer for
my father's question.
Six years of silence
had made us strangers . . .
no common language . . .
no grounds whereon
the minds could meet . . .
no shared vocabulary
of accepted definitions . . .
no latitude for the palsied
two-step we must dance
until we found the rhythm
that could unite us in
a pavane of mutual respect
and understanding.

Lost my faith?
That's all he could imagine
that could have made me change
my way. My crime?
Fourteen years of schooling
and practice had failed
to make of me the minister
of my parents' dreams.

I had not lost my faith.
I knew exactly where I put it.
I had not lost anything;
I had found the person
I was always meant to be.

My father did not wish
to talk about that.
so we never did,
and I went on my way
without his company.

He had had only one dream
for me. Sadly, for both
of us, it was
the wrong
one.

FORGIVENESS

It has been forty years
since my father died.
Last night I let him go.
I forgave him his crimes
against me, his failures
at loving.

I did not forgive because,
"After all," some said, "he was
doing the best he knew."
Somehow intentions
did not seem
to count.

Nor because he deserved
forgiveness. He never wanted it.
No, I forgave because
my tanks are empty
of the righteous fuel
of anger.

Forgiveness does not seek excuses.
Forgiveness happens, sometimes,
when the truth is so awful
that there simply is
nothing else that
one can do.

THE COMING NIGHT

The darkness came . . .
I escaped . . .
the darkness
remained

THE DARKNESS CAME . . .

Mid-October evening, nineteen sixty-three;
small segregated southern town;
night coming on, but no street light,
where the Klansmen came for me;
five of them, advancing, resolute,
in darkened Buick,
fueled by fear-based anger
aimed at me.

(I had said the wrong things from the pulpit)

Dark times in fear-filled town,
dark street with no one around
but me and them.
Their darkness . . .
town's darkness . . .
about to descend
on me.

I saw it coming;
I saw the trap they planned:
my regular turn for home . . .
a stop sign at the corner . . . .
They would get there first, and wait,
blocking my way. . . and
they had not come
for a polite exchange of views.

What they had come for never happened;
I took a different route, so . . .
my windshield was not smashed;
I was not dragged from my car;
I was not beaten with their clubs;
I was not left broken in the street,
clothed in bruises, my blood
pooling on the pavement.

Tricked out of their prey,
they parked across the street,
from my house, and waited . . .
still nurturing their hatred,
hoping I'd come out again.

I didn't, of course.
The six of us left to imagine
the violence that did not occur . . . .
They, no doubt, with bitterness
and simmering frustration
(why did they never try again?),
I with shuddering relief
at having barely missed
what might have been done.

The darkness came . . .
I escaped . . .
the darkness
remained . . . .

THREE MEN

Three men;
unheard of men with names
we did not want to know;
three invisible men,
lit by one dark light;
cold men burning;
outsiders from the inside out,
lost in a clear intent.

Three men;
known by us all;
incarnations of our hopes;
three public men, outlined
in dream's floodlights;
prescient prophets,
compass bearers to
a nation's tomorrow.

Three men:
Lee Harvey . . . ,
Sirhan . . . ,
James Earl . . . .

Three men:
John Fitzgerald . . . ,
Robert Francis . . . ,
Martin Luther . . . .

Three men,
three giants gleaming
with the promise
of their dreams
for us.

Three men,
three tiny hopeless men
desperate to murder
their own anonymity
with a gun.

Three men died.
Three men killed.
What need compels
the street sparrow
to hate the eagle,
the hopeless to destroy
the dreamer of big dreams?

ABSOLUTION

He was my friend, a mentor, and a minister
I would have been glad to emulate;
warm, bright, sure in his belief, but
softly spoken . . . a family man: devoted wife,
two teenaged kids . . . and the popular pastor
of a mid-sized suburban church.

He was not a powerful orator, and yet,
people listened when he spoke, and
all who knew him, knew him as one to watch . . .
saw in his future a tall steepled First Church
in some metropolis . . . a leadership role
in his beloved denomination. They knew
he could not help but make it to the top.

But what they did *not* know was that,
beneath his clerical garb, disguised by the
the seeming comfort of his easy-going piety,
he wore a secret he never could reveal:
at some stage on the path to middle-age
he had realized that he was gay.

The word *gay*, of course, was not
in common usage yet. Back then
the cruder *queer* was the label applied
to one who is emotionally and sexually
drawn to one of his same gender,
and it always cast the scarlet shadow
of rejection and disgrace.

And what was he to do? He could not
beg forgiveness for what then seemed
unforgivable. And, anyway, did not forgiveness
first need penitence? And did not penitence mean,
in this case, changing who he was?
And that, he knew, he could not do.

But . . . maybe . . .
he could change the terms
of his disgrace . . . .

And maybe he could give his loved ones,
at the very least, a different
sort of pain
to bear . . .

. . . and perhaps,
for himself?
a different sort of
absolution . . . ?

. . . as he pressed the muzzle of the pistol
to his head. . . .

....

This poem is dedicated to the memory
of a man whom I admired and respected,
and who will remain anonymous.

THE WILD THINGS

. . . a life term of wonder
at my old courageous world,
that it should have
such creatures in it.

THE BIRDS

They came for me,
the birds,
in my fifteenth summer.
The fighting now ended, we had moved
from sooty wartime Birmingham,
second floor apartment,
to peacetime suburban bungalow,
with yard, and -
beyond the fence - a wildness
of undeveloped woods.

Pictures in a child's book
had forged no connection
to the birds that thronged
the urban streets:
the constant common pigeons,
hoodlum Starlings,
ubiquitous English Sparrows,
whose colors, like every other
natural thing in that
unnatural city,
were dulled by fallout
from the foundries.

Now spilling into
my new backyard . . .
a fallout of a different sort:
a pulsing cascade of
flashing color,
through the water oaks and pines,

and amidst the undergrowth
and fallen leaves,
a kaleidoscopic dance
to the syncopated rhythm
of an unblended chorus
of avian polyphony.

I recognized a few of them:
Cardinals . . . Robins . . .
Mockingbirds . . . Blue Jays . . . .
But most of them were new,
and I was caught . . .
arrested . . .
held captive . . .
convicted of my ignorance,
and sentenced, right then and there,
to a life term of wonder
at my old courageous world,
that it should have
such creatures in it.

Seven decades later,
I am captivated still,
and still
fifteen.

GULF SHORES - FRIGATEBIRDS

Four of them came this year,
the Frigatebirds. Like crooked
crosses of some celtic sect,
they stand in the air, in defiance
of an approaching storm.

Hundreds of feet above the beach,
they hover at an altitude far
higher than the homing gulls
and pelicans can reach.

Like four kites straining at
invisible strings, solemn,
immobile, not flying, being
flown by the wind, they hang
facing straight into
the freshening breeze.

In a box formation, one
at each corner of the square,
with hardly a movement of wings,
they slide sideways down the beach
to the west, a hundred yards or so,
then back again, several times,
until they vanish into a setting sun.

Black, ominous, other-worldly,
members of an alien, avian clan,
totally at ease in their element.

Like their namesake ships,
they are the masters
of the coming storm.

A TENNESSEE AUGUST AFTERNOON

A Tennessee August afternoon,
the sunlight's angle narrowing,
the aging hackberry trees transformed
by the almost horizontal rays, turning
them into green, stained-glass walls;
the backyard a vespers chapel,
suitable for the sacred chorale,
a polyphonic fugue of July Flies
blessing the day past, welcoming
the night, their palpitating rhythm
slowing with the coming dark . . .
to one last voice, to one
dying note, to one
unqualified
Amen.

A DANCE OF WINTER TREES

Windy night,
bare winter trees,
black lace against
a fading sky.

Shifting, overlapped limbs,
agitated branches
wringing twiggy fingers
in nervous anticipation.

Sapless veins,
inky leafless promises
dancing hopefully,
in slate-draped ballroom

a skeletal pavane?
a twilight progress
to mourn last years lost fruit
and green cloak's molting?

Or a lenten pause
before the call to regenerate?
just one last celebration,
one last country reel,

before the weight of leaves,
the annual pregnancy of green,
the holy seed-making duty
of sacred photosynthesis?

THE RUBY-THROAT

A Ruby-throated Hummingbird
poses problems for a poet,
because there is nothing comparable
in the world of birds (and poets are
always comparing things) except
another hummingbird, so what's
to say? I suppose I could report -
like a TV sport's announcer -
that it is "very unique", but
I was an English major and
I know better
than that.

Or perhaps I should stick to
the facts: how small it is:
one to one and two tenths of an ounce;
or how fast: in normal flight?
about twenty-five miles an hour;
with a wing beat of sixty to eighty
strokes a second. But numbers
cannot begin to explain
the wonder of the one I met
one april morning on
Dauphin Island,
Alabama.

He landed on the low reach
of a trumpet vine, about four feet
from me, and looked me in the eye,
with no apparent alarm;

and then
I'll swear I
heard
him
say,

"Sir, would you just back off
and give me some quiet time
and a little space? You see,
I've been flying since yesterday
about this time, with nothing to eat,
and nowhere to stop, across
the Gulf of Mexico, more than
five hundred miles (the rainstorm
a hundred miles out of Yucatan
didn't help) and I just need to rest
and take in a bit of energy;
then I'll be
heading
north
again . . . ."

I quietly backed
away.

I THINK THAT THERE ARE RABBITS

I think that there are rabbits
living under my neighbor's tool shed
(a scene, almost, from a Beatrix Potter book).

I've seen them come and go,
at least one adult, some juveniles
(none were wearing clothes, or little leather shoes).

I did meet one one day when he was
munching dandelions in my yard.
I spoke in passing; it seemed polite.

He didn't reply, just twitched his nose at me,
as if deciding whether to introduce himself.
I'm glad he didn't think it necessary.

If he had said to me, "Hi, my name is Peter,
who are you?" I doubt that I would ever be able
to set my foot again in my backyard.

THE LOON

Out on the morning sea,
concealed amid the wealth
of sparkling sun diamonds,
laid down by dawning rays,
a welcome to a lonely traveler;
an uncommon
Common
Loon.

This odd assemblage of choices,
from Darwin's natural selections,
will not sing his loon songs
for me tonight; his
singing place
a far off
northern
lake.

Come dark, he must be on his way;
the future of his kind
awaits him up there. It is
for her, and her alone
and there, and only there
that his heart will
find its
song.

THE CROW'S ALARM

The Crow,
having spied a Red-tail
in the top of a large oak tree,
instinctively attacks -
but only verbally, of course -
"Craw! Craw!
Craw, craw, craw!",
calling for reinforcements,
but, from just beyond the perimeter
of the hawk's effective reach
(Crows are not dumb).

The only response to his alarm,
on this day, comes
from his little cousin, Jay,
who also from a distance
(Jays are not stupid, either),
eggs on his larger relative
with his nagging, "Do it!
Do it, do it!"

The Red-tail seems not at all
ruffled by all this to-do . . .
if only they'd shut up and
go away, maybe he could
concentrate on the squirrel
ambling stupidly (they are)
across an open expanse of yard,

seemingly unaware that he
is close to becoming the lunch
of a very large, and
very hungry
bird.

All in the natural
order of things.

A CONGRESS OF BLUE JAYS

The neighborhood Blue Jays
are holding some sort of congress,
on some issue of importance
to the local population.

There are questions to be
discussed and voted upon, and
there are - as with most questions -
at least two sides.

There are the *pros*, who are
calling out with monotonous insistency,
in a silly sounding sing-song,
"Do it! Do it! Do it!"

And the *cons*, who are
shouting angrily in a volume
designed to drown the opposition,
"Nay! Nay! Nay!"

No one is keeping order and,
like similar human conclaves,
no one is listening to the other side
(they could use a copy of *Roberts Rules*).

RE-IMAGINING GOD

. . . a heart's song to
the glory of
Green-life,
to the mystery of
God-life . . .
to the wonder of
being in it.

WHENEVER I HEAR THE WORD GOD

Whenever I hear the word God,
a number of images light up: one
of an elderly, grandfatherly type,
puttering about in his flower bed,
smiling encouragement to his blooms,
gently frowning at invasive weeds,
while humming softly to himself.

Why a grandfatherly sort? Well, think.
What do grandfathers do? Not much.
No need to work; their days of earning
mostly past, like God's creative burst.
He set off some big explosions in
His inventive youth, but all
of that has been done.

Still, God is much too powerful
to be, at his age, going about
actually doing things. He can't
be changing stuff for every prayerful
Tom, Dick, or Dorothy. His own
established laws of physics
would soon protest.

Now back to our retired Grandfather
as a metaphor for God. What is it
that grandfathers do the best?
They love unconditionally. They don't
command, or threaten punishment,
or discriminate amongst their own.

They love; that's all.

But some would say that to think
of God as an elderly man
with nothing much to do
would make Him totally irrelevant
and useless as a God. Really?
A God whose only job is to
love us unconditionally? Irrelevant?
Really?

(As a footnote: Some feminists
among us might protest that HE
should be thought of as a SHE.
Well, O.K., I don't mind thinking of
God as a grandmotherly sort,
puttering about in Her garden,
with nothing to do but love).

LISTENING EXPECTANTLY

If you listen very carefully,
and quietly and, yes, expectantly,
you just may hear the voice of God

singing. He is singing
to Himself . . . and to you and me,
of course, but mostly to Himself.

He is singing a song of birth,
a song of His own birth, for
being born is what God does.

He is constantly coming to life;
coming to life in the earth-forms
of His creation, breathing His life

into the green world of His planting,
into the animated world of His husbandry.
His songs are lyrical without lyrics.

They are not anthems, or hymns, or psalms.
The only sounds His singing knows
are the sounds of life coming to life,

His life and the joy of being in it.
Listen . . .
Quietly . . .
Expectantly . . . .
And you shall hear God's song.

THE BOTANICAL SYMPHONY

Here's a question for you
that has been bothering me.
Why is it that we cannot hear
the green world growing,
the grass, the weeds, the trees?
Why don't they make a sound?

Take that sapling Shingle Oak
that volunteered in my backyard;
it's growing tall at an even rate
of about two feet a year, while
also making brand new leaves
each spring, plus new stems and
branches to hang them on.

Wouldn't you think that
all of that productivity would
make some kind of noise?

Then, there is the sap
that's moving beneath the bark
of the Hackberry tree
outside my kitchen door.
It's carrying nutrients from the soil
up to the photosynthetical
factory in its crown.

You'd think there would be
some auditory evidence
of all that busyness.

Every sort of living plant,
from tallest tree to tiniest flower,
has something going on
inside of it, some movement,
some reaction, some process
on which its life depends.

Is it reasonable then to assume
that all those fibrous machinations
occur in a sonic vacuum?

And what would we hear,
if we could find a way
to amplify those green
reverberations? Would we be
an enraptured audience
at a formal concert of some
grand botanical symphony?

Or would we just find ourselves
eavesdropping on God, again,
an old man quietly
singing to himself.

RADNOR LAKE - MORNING AFTER RAIN

Late June,
a morning after rain,
sun glinting through trees,
rising moisture making
slanted shafts
of light.

All is still;
the forest hesitates to stir,
to throw off evening's chill.
All is waiting;
the color of expectancy,
it would seem,
is green.

Green is everywhere;
green has dominion.
Mother Earth, the queen,
is robed in green.
Green-life is . . .
God-life?

The woods resound
with sounds birds make,
like punctuation marks
in Green-life's
(in God-life's?)
self-expression.

And music bursts
from Cardinals and Carolinas.
The wonder of Green-life
(of God-life), the joy
of being in it,
celebrated
by song.

I pen these words,
a heart's song to
the glory of
Green-life,
to the mystery of
God-life . . .
to the wonder of
being
in it.

SACRED BOOKS

The title of this poem bothers me
(I guess that's why I'm writing it);
I find that I am troubled by
the very notion of a *sacred book.*

Take that volume on my shelf, all bound
in black morocco, all edges gilt,
with the word *Holy* stamped upon its spine;
that book makes me sort of nervous.

I think that's because so many people
take that title seriously, believing
that the book we call the *Bible*
contains somehow the very word of God.

Well, that is a dangerous supposition.
For ages obviously fallible men, who armed
themselves with *God's infallible Book*,
have committed some of history's vilest crimes.

Sacred books have spawned holy wars, crusades
and righteous inquisitions. And even today,
another *sacred book* is telling angry desert men
just whose contrary heads to lop.

Isn't it time we let God off the hook
as the ghost-writer of all those
testaments, commandments, epistles,
prophesies, and gospels?

He didn't write all that stuff.
It was written by humans just like us,
whose DNA, just like ours,
did not contain the holiness gene.

who, like us, were just
trying to figure things out.

LIFE (LARGE L)

This brief expression of,
incarnation of, Life (large L),
that I call I, me,
my life (small l),
is now mostly finished,
my allotted paragraph
on its last sentence now.
Soon it will come to . . .
period . . . full stop;
then . . .

    The End

of life, mine (small l);
not Life (large L).
Life (large L)
does not, cannot, end . . .
is forever . . .
goes on saying itself
forever, every living thing
a paragraph
(a sentence, a phrase)
spoken by, incarnation of
Life (large L). It goes on
giving shape to itself,
forever . . . that Process being
the Source of all life (small l).

Our small minds, not
understanding who, or what
we were, pictured Life (large L),
the Process, the Source,
as someone like ourselves,
named it in our image,
our metaphor, made
it small, like us,

even gave it our pronoun.

Why not call the ultimate
Source, the ultimate Process
what it is . . . ?
Life (large L).

BEDTIME PRAYER

So, now I lay me down to sleep,
and let me lie in quiet deep.
I cannot pray the Lord to keep;
who cannot have what I cannot give.
And if I die before I wake,
then when I die I will not wake.
And if I wake, then I must wait
to live and die another day,
when I will lay me down to sleep,
in doubt there is a Lord to keep;
or that there is a soul to give or take;
just me and all my promises,
some that I've kept, and
some that I've faked.
That's all, so if it please, then
let me just lie down,
and let me
simply sleep.
Amen.

THE HINGING MOMENT

It was the hinging moment,
the, perhaps, millennium measured
moment of turning . . .
from one thing to another,
from one life to another,
from several beings to one someone new;
not of a sudden, not in one giant step toward man
across the chasm dividing then from now,
before from after;
a slow, piecemeal, ratcheting, hesitant,
doubtful progress it was,
this birth of adventure,
with no choice but to go.

Something had said, "Wake up!
Open your eyes! Look around!"
What was it?
Something prodding, tickling, whispering,
"Time to get up."
Just a hint of dawn at first,
to trouble the sleep of eons,
a worrisome disturbance of the peace?
But then! . . . a rising sun,
a brightness of never noticed color!
New contrasts, comparisons,
likenesses, understandings;
light is to warmth as dark is to cold;
repetitions, rhythms,
seasons changing, warm to cold, life to death.

The warmth comes back, rebirth;
again and again, count on it;
a beat, a pulsing pattern.
A pattern . . . curious . . . .
What's the connection?
An urge to know more.
Had all this been there all along,
and we just never noticed
during our billion year trek
from Trilobite to this transition Man?

And what a time it must have been
when our new species roused itself.
Imagine how it was for our first kin
in those new dawning days;
how it was in the beginning
to be the first
to question who
am I? . . . are you? . . . are we?
To question why . . . what if . . .
what else . . . what next;
to muse upon tomorrow . . .
to brood about what used to be,
and ask what will, consider
something different than what is,
a life not just like this,
another time than this today,
to hope for the best, to fret about the worst;
the first to think of life and death
together in one life,
to wonder what it's all about,
to question what it means.

Here was the miracle:
a creature had arrived who stood apart,
not because he was the best,
or different on first glance,
a God, immortal, no . . .
but just because he could -
stand apart, that is -
step out of the passing march, and
watch himself go by.
And with that objectivity,
and that imagination,
was born Time,
History, Meaning, Spirit,
Morality, Art, Science,
all that would ennoble us
To reach beyond our grasp.

WHAT'S WRONG WITH THE WORLD?

What's wrong with the world?
I'll tell you; it's no mystery.
What's wrong is this: Human Beings
are more interested in God and
in being right than they are
in Queen Anne's Lace,
Swallow-tailed Butterflies,
and Carolina Wrens. And
I'm not sure that
can be fixed.

FURTHER DISCOVERIES

. . . it's no one's fault; it can't be helped;
it's just the un-square dance we dance,
the morality play we constantly re-enact.

PARENTAL FAILINGS

Mother-guilt, father-guilt;
parental failings our inheritance.
We leave our children what Mom and Pop -
their Grannies - passed on to us,
and theirs to them, and what
our kids, in turn, will give to theirs.
It's no one's fault; it can't be helped;
it's just the un-square dance we dance,
the morality play we constantly perform.

Just don't take it all too seriously;
it isn't called *The Human Comedy* for naught.

AUTHORSHIP

I wrote a book.
It was published.
A few people read it,
mostly friends and kin.
They seemed to like it,
the ones who let me know.
Only one plainly said
she highly disapproved,
but knowing her, I didn't mind.
It was a book about God,
and He didn't seem to mind
that what I said about Him
was not especially complimentary.
Or maybe the truth was that
the scarcity of royalties
was just the joke He
played on me while
letting me know
just who is
in charge.

IMMORTALITY

I know where I am going when I die,
and it isn't to Heaven, and certainly
not to Hell. No, it's already been arranged;
when I die, I'm going back to school.

And not just any school, and not -
God forbid - to earn another useless degree.
I am going to Medical School, and . . .
I am going there to teach.

I have already been appointed
an Instructor of Anatomy, albeit
a rather passive and a very silent
one, because I shall be dead.

But I am very proud to celebrate
my future life as a lifeless cadaver,
a body preserved for dissection
by some precocious M.D. to be.

I hope she (or he) will find me to be
a useful (certainly cooperative) subject,
capable of disclosing much that is important
about the history of one physical human life.

She will see with her own eyes, up close,
what teenage smoking does to elderly lungs;
how radioactive implants effect a prostate gland;
and how a heart recovers from by-pass surgery.

And so much more than I could possibly foresee.
Lives could be saved, if indirectly, because
of me. That surely is life after death,
a quietly satisfying immortality.

GULF SHORES ICARUS

On the beach a glamorous *Icarus*,
wearing a pair of wings,
elegantly fledged,
a baroque angel's appendages.
Alas, only a tattoo, but
a real work of art, a bold statement,
covering her back from nape
down to where the primaries' tips
softly caress the outer curves
of exquisitely generous cheeks.

The back straps of her bikini -
top and bottom - look like a harness
of sorts, designed to hold
her wings in place, feeding the fantasy:
to unfurl them and take flight
she would have to be completely nude.
Unfortunately, the authorities, I suspect,
would frown upon a naked angel
practicing her aerobatics
over a beach meant for family fun.

BEING RIGHT

Being right is often wrong,
perfection is a curse;
moralism is such a bore,
but righteousness is worse.

Sin's a guilt producing word,
but feeling guilty does no good;
You're better off with what you like,
than all that stuff you think you should.

Normality is a burden,
fitting in's a backside pain;
conformity is a useless chore,
with nothing much to gain.

Heaven's an empty promise,
and Hell's an empty threat;
you say you want what you deserve?
Be thankful it's not what you get.

So be good or be bad,
or be right or be wrong;
but never steal some other's oughts,
or sing someone else's song.

ON SUN BLUE TEMPERED DAYS

At seven on sun blue, tempered days
(the coffee cup's still warm),
Miss Janie walks the winter sands,
the first of the old ones
to print her sneakers among bird tracks,
where sodden feathers sprout
in place of summer's cans.

Herding reluctant pipers, she prods the rows
of washed coquina jewels,
sand mounted by the chiseling surf,
hunting the aged comber's gold.
This slanted street of precious stones
leads back today to memories of pantaloons
and fantasies of choiring conchs.

So, singing the sea's first song,
she rises on a herring's wings
to stand a chance against the homing tide.
Then, bending back to beach
she pokes a few more piles, and turns to cottage.
The wind is rising now;
the coffee cup is cold.

THE BOARDWALK AT HUNTINGTON

The boardwalk at Huntington,
a wooden peninsula, thrusting,
like a printed invitation,
out into the tidal marsh;

this brackish Eden, obedient
to the phases of the moon,
holds out to us today
a promise of connection;

a fecund soup of sandy mud,
decaying life and tall cordgrass,
the ocean's teeming nursery
where sea-life comes to spawn;

a reminder of our own beginnings,
when, at some primordial dawning,
an evolving predecessor crawled
out of a similar soup, onto the land,

and decided to stay.

IMPROMPTU ON THE BEACH

It was late afternoon,
the bathers and sun worshipers
mostly gone to cottage,
when the kid with a violin
tucked 'neath his chin
strode down the strand.

Shoes abandoned, pants
rolled up, he began to dance
a splashing two-step
in the shallow surf,
while playing
his own accompaniment.

Against the muffled counterpoint
of low tide's rolling breakers
he dipped and turned and swayed
in rhythm with the sawing
of his bow.

Eyes closed, hearing only
the violin's voice, blending with
the spirit's inner urgency,
he played his own unscored
sonata of pure joy.

As I said,
he was only
a teenaged kid . . .

But I was listening,
uninvited,
to his certain future.

SETTING THINGS STRAIGHT

Everyone who knows me
knows I spent ten years
as a Presbyterian Minister,
fourteen, if you count the time
I spent in the seminary
training to be God's man.

Why did I give it up?
Many would ask about my
Crisis of Faith; but I'm sorry,
I don't have much to say
along those lines; the truth
is far more pedestrian:

I just didn't like the work,
or the example I was supposed
to set. I didn't enjoy what
I was called upon to do, and
I didn't much care for those
I was called upon to serve.

It was that simple, and
I am quite satisfied that God,
for one, was pleased as punch
that I did not agonize
over my *calling*,
or try to tough it out,

but simply moved on
to what came next.

LITURGY FOR A CHRISTMAS EVE

A month ago, on Christmas Eve,
Gregory Armistead Connors, the Third,
the children down, his wife out back,
got up from his fireside couch,
and picked the biggest brightest ball
from off the imitation tree.

He pulled the pin
(like John Wayne, with his teeth),
and flung it at the world,
exploding reality into a
hundred reduced images,
perceptions brightly reflected
in minute shards of concave glass.

He bent to the destruction, made faces,
laughed at what he saw,
and then, with total satisfaction
at his powers of un-creation,
Greg Connors swept it all -
broken mirrors, world, reality,
reflections of himself -
in among the ashes of burnt oak.

TWO AUTUMNS

What really happens is,
before they turn to brown, curl up and fall,
green leaves turn red,
then yellow; their intensity of hues
pertains to recent rain, timely frost,
and slowing down of circulating juice.

Those maple leaves are not aflame,
nor touched by special radiance,
nor reflect the burnished excellence of God.
They're only dying now,
for that's the way it is:
all colors change, preparing for long sleep.

The same will happen soon to me,
when cold comes on and circulating fluid slows.
But I shall turn pale gray, a non-reflective shade
that no one hails
(one wonders if fall's
fevered leaves evoke the forest's praise).

But still some folks insist
on seeing God
in flaming maple leaves.
If so, then I insist
they see him also
in my fading flesh . . .
in the natural order of things.

LENDA

. . . to join the chorus of those who knew her gentle ways of making us feel good about ourselves.

I WANT TO WRITE A POEM . . .

I want to write a poem about
how beautiful she was, how wise
and loving, and filled with grace.

. . . to praise the things she loved,
rocks, clouds, stars, the grays of
winter trees, the *Oystercatcher* birds.

. . . to hum the visual music that
she wrote with threads, the colors
that sang her private songs.

. . . to laugh with her at sandals
in winter, the five pillows she
slept with, her addiction to lemons.

. . . to celebrate her questing mind,
her love of books, need to know,
intolerance of stupidity.

. . . to join the chorus of those who
knew her gentle way of making us
feel better about ourselves.

. . . to salute her courage, her
decision in the end, not to rage,
but to step freely into night.

I will write this poem one day, but first
I must put down, by writing it down,
my sadness at her leaving.

THE USEFULNESS OF SEVERED STRANDS

The usefulness
of the severed strands
of a piece of string . . .

the price we put on the contents
of an empty box . . .

the literary quality
of a book's end papers . . .

the desired destination
of a road that simply ends . . .

the meaning of my beloved's death . . .
the severing;
the emptiness;
the blankness;
the premature end;

the meaning?

No.

HOLES

The house I live in
is full of holes.
They don't leak weather;
I can't see through them
to the open sky.

These are holes
in the inner space,
empty places left
unfilled by departure;
holes where no one is
who once was there.

There is no one here
who purchased half the books
that line our shelves.

The other side of the
breakfast table is only
an empty space.

Half the king-sized bed
is never occupied.

There is a huge void upstairs
where once was an artist's studio

There are drawers in chests
that are merely
sliding empty boxes.

It is strange how often
one finds oneself
conversing
with an empty hole.

TO A DEAR FRIEND

Dear friend,
you had been there
all along. I had been
waiting for you
to show up and
tell me your
name.

A SECOND CHANCE

When we started,
what I thought
would surely be,
was not then
what I thought
it was,
and so became
what might have been,
and as such
never could.

What I think
I see this time
is something that
I feel is new,
or something that
I didn't see before,
and so might become
something that
could really be.

RECOGNITION

No, not that nonsense about
the heels over the head, nor falling in . . .
and at the first seeing. The thing is
the initial sight was not like
a first time. At least
it did not feel
that way
to me.

I had seen you many times before,
in my mind . . . next door . . . down the street
at a distance, or sitting next to me -
I don't remember where - conversing brightly,
perhaps in an unformed dream . . .
or in the words of
a song projected
on my heart from
somewhere far
and close.

That is why the first time
we met that day, I already knew . . . ;
no need to fall, or do a loop.
I recognized you. Dear friend.
You had been there all along.
I had been waiting for you
to step up
and tell me
your
name.

WHILE THERE STILL IS LIGHT

So crown the day,
the sun has passed its zenith;
this afternoon of months and years
becomes my new domain.

So come and sit with me,
while there is yet reflective green,
before the graying of the palette,
before the blurring of the lines.

I will not expect of you that
you should stay my night;
you will know when you must go,
but while there still is light . . .

there are birdsongs . . .
there are flowers . . .
and there are sunlit clouds . . . .
There is art . . .
and there is poetry . . . .

EPILOGUE

. . . a festival of incarnation . . . .

IN THE MEANTIME . . .

We are all invited
to a Festival of Incarnation,
a celebration of the embodiment
of the divine Life of the Universe
in all the myriad forms
in which and through which
that Life (Large L) expresses itself . . .
including you and me
and every other being
that has life (little L).

CPSIA information can be obtained
at www.ICGtesting.com
Printed in the USA
LVOW11s0003170517
534792LV00001B/100/P

9 780692 837535